The British Medical Association

INDIGESTION & ULCERS

PROFESSOR C. J. HAWKEY AND DR. N. J. D. WIGHT

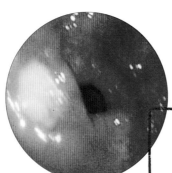

MEDICAL EDITOR
DR. TONY SMITH

A DORLING KINDERSLEY BOOK

IMPORTANT

This book is not designed as a substitute for personal medical advice but as a supplement to that advice for the patient who wishes to understand more about his/her condition.

Before taking any form of treatment **YOU SHOULD ALWAYS CONSULT YOUR MEDICAL PRACTITIONER.**

In particular (without limit) you should note that advances in medical science occur rapidly and some of the information contained in this book about drugs and treatment may very soon be out of date.

PLEASE NOTE

The author regrets that he cannot enter into any correspondence with readers.

DORLING KINDERSLEY

LONDON, NEW YORK, AUCKLAND, DELHI, JOHANNESBURG, MUNICH, PARIS AND SYDNEY

DK www.dk.com

Senior Editors Nicki Lampon, Mary Lindsay
Senior Designers Jan English, Sarah Hall
Production Controller Elizabeth Cherry

Managing Editor Martyn Page
Managing Art Editor Bryn Walls

Produced for Dorling Kindersley Limited by Design Revolution, Queens Park Villa, 30 West Drive, Brighton, East Sussex BN2 2GE
Editorial Director Ian Whitelaw
Art Director Becky Willis
Editor Zak Knowles
Designer Andrew Easton

Published in Great Britain in 2000 by
Dorling Kindersley Limited,
9 Henrietta Street, London WC2E 8PS

2 4 6 8 10 9 7 5 3 1

A CIP catalogue record for this book is available from the British Library

ISBN 07513 08412

Reproduced by Colourscan, Singapore
Printed in Hong Kong by Wing King Tong

Contents

INTRODUCTION 7

NORMAL DIGESTION 10

TREATING INDIGESTION YOURSELF 16

DO YOU NEED TO SEE YOUR DOCTOR? 25

GASTRO-OESOPHAGEAL REFLUX 40

PEPTIC ULCERS AND *Helicobacter pylori* 55

TREATING A PEPTIC ULCER 69

NON-ULCER DYSPEPSIA 74

STOMACH CANCER 79

USEFUL ADDRESSES 84

INDEX 85

ACKNOWLEDGEMENTS 88

Introduction

Virtually everyone has had indigestion at some time, and for most people it is simply a minor nuisance. More often than not, it happens when you have overindulged in food or alcohol or eaten something that does not agree with you, and it only lasts for a relatively short time.

In these situations, you can either wait for the symptoms to subside or treat yourself with a remedy from the pharmacist without needing to see a doctor.

FAST FOOD
Eating while standing up or in a hurry can result in the temporary symptoms of indigestion, but more serious symptoms should be investigated.

For some people, however, symptoms of indigestion can be persistent and so severe that they can interfere with everyday life. Symptoms may be caused by some undiagnosed problem within the digestive system that needs to be properly identified and, if necessary, treated by a doctor. The purpose of this book is to help you distinguish between minor symptoms that you can safely treat yourself with the advice of a pharmacist and those that need further investigation and may require you to visit your doctor.

The word 'indigestion' means different things to different people, but mostly it is used to describe discomfort in the central upper abdomen related in

WHICH MEDICATION?
If you only suffer indigestion occasionally, your pharmacist will be able to offer you advice on which treatments are most appropriate.

some way to eating or swallowing. Other common symptoms include:

- Pain in the chest or abdomen.
- A burning sensation in the chest (heartburn) often linked with food or with liquid coming up into the throat or the back of the mouth (known medically as gastro-oesophageal reflux).
- Belching or burping gas or wind into the mouth.

If you only get such symptoms of indigestion occasionally, you should ask your local pharmacist about over-the-counter treatments, which can be used safely to treat the odd bout of indigestion. You should also read the section in this book on lifestyle changes (see p.17) and make any necessary changes to reduce your chances of further attacks. Such simple measures will be all that are needed to solve the problem in many cases, but, if they have not worked after a couple of weeks, or if you start getting symptoms for the first time in your life when you are over 40, you should make an appointment with your GP. Severe or persistent symptoms may be caused by a more serious underlying problem – such as a peptic ulcer, for example – and the sooner it is diagnosed and treated, the better. Many more powerful remedies are available only on prescription; these are explained in detail starting on p.69.

There is no point in putting up with unpleasant symptoms for any longer than you have to, so, if self-help does not work, do not hesitate to consult your doctor. See your doctor straight away if, as well as having indigestion, you have also lost your appetite and are losing weight as a result, if you feel constantly sick (even if you do not vomit) or if you have any of the symptoms listed on pp.25–27, as these could mean that you need urgent treatment.

KEY POINTS

- Indigestion is extremely common, affecting most people at some time in their life.
- Symptoms are usually minor and can easily be treated at home.
- Some symptoms are more important and require evaluation by a doctor.
- This book will help you to treat yourself and also help you to decide if it is necessary to see your doctor.

Normal digestion

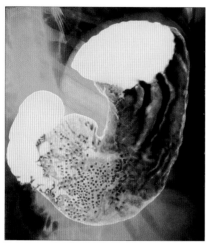

Many people have only the vaguest idea of the size, shape, position and function of the stomach and the other digestive organs.This chapter starts with a brief outline of the normal process of digestion and what each of the main parts of the digestive system does. If this is all familiar to you, just go straight to pp.13–14, where the main types of indigestion are described.

A KEY ELEMENT
The stomach, which lies below and behind the liver, is an essential element in the digestive system, storing and helping to break down the food that we eat.

To extract nutrients from the food we eat we need to digest it. First the food has to be changed into a liquid or semi-liquid form. Then, complex substances such as fats and proteins have to be broken down into smaller chemical units that can be absorbed through the walls of the intestine into the bloodstream.

The process of digestion begins in the mouth, where the teeth and tongue chop large pieces of food into smaller ones. The salivary glands release saliva into the mouth to mix with the food. Saliva makes it easier to move food round to chew, and it also contains an enzyme called salivary amylase that starts to digest carbohydrates such as sugars and starches. Saliva is slightly acid and, when you are not eating, it goes on being produced and

The Digestive Apparatus

Ingested food passes down the oesophagus and into the stomach, where it is churned and mixed thoroughly with digestive juices secreted by the stomach lining. Further digestive enzymes are added to the food in the duodenum.

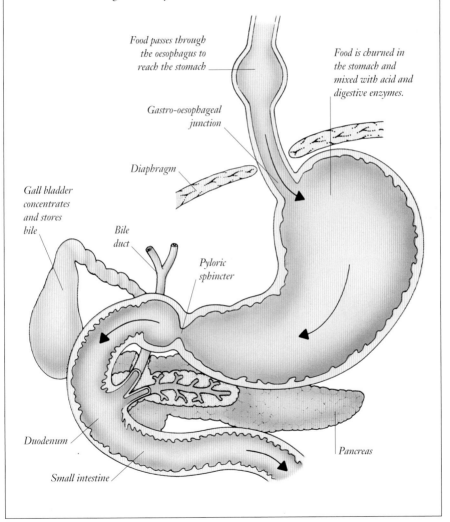

Food passes through the oesophagus to reach the stomach

Food is churned in the stomach and mixed with acid and digestive enzymes.

Gastro-oesophageal junction

Diaphragm

Gall bladder concentrates and stores bile

Bile duct

Pyloric sphincter

Duodenum

Small intestine

Pancreas

helps to keep your mouth and teeth clean and stop plaque developing on your teeth. People who have conditions in which salivary production is reduced often experience a dry mouth, difficulty swallowing and increased tooth decay.

Once the food is chewed and softened in the mouth, the tongue pushes it to the back of the throat, where muscles propel it down the oesophagus (gullet). The food passes from the oesophagus into the stomach through a muscular one-way valve, called the lower oesophageal sphincter, which prevents the contents of

The Functions of the Stomach

The stomach is a muscular J-shaped sac that forms the widest part of the digestive tract. It has three main functions in the digestive process, and these are listed below.

- It acts as a storage container, so that we can swallow all the food needed for many hours within a few minutes.

- It plays a large part in the physical and chemical processes of digestion. Food in the stomach is churned and crushed, although you notice this only when the activity is excessive because your stomach does not contain the same number of sensory nerves as other parts of the body, such as the skin. Glands within the stomach lining produce a powerful acid and enzymes that help to break down the constituents of food into simpler chemical compounds. The walls of the stomach are normally protected against acid attack by a layer of protective mucus, but, if this is reduced or damaged, an ulcer may form. The oesophagus does not have this protective lining and so is more easily damaged by acid.

- Food may stay in the stomach for several hours, and during this time the stomach acid will destroy most of the bacteria and other micro-organisms that may have contaminated it. Very little is absorbed directly into the bloodstream through the stomach walls, apart from a few substances such as alcohol and aspirin.

the stomach from being forced back into the oesophagus when the stomach contracts or you lie flat. The stomach has three main functions, shown in the box opposite.

Eventually the liquidised food is pushed onwards through another valve, the pylorus, into the duodenum, the first few inches of the small intestine. Here, further chemicals are added to neutralise the stomach acid, together with enzymes from the pancreas to help to digest carbohydrates, fats and proteins, and bile from the liver to help to digest fats. The digested food then passes into the remaining 20 feet (six metres) of small intestine, so called because, although it is long, its diameter is smaller than that of the large intestine. The chemical breakdown is completed in the small intestine and the chemical constituents of the meal are absorbed into the blood and lymphatic vessels.

The main tasks of the large intestine are to reabsorb the water that is used in digestion and to eliminate the undigested food and fibre.

WHAT CAN GO WRONG?

Almost everyone experiences occasional attacks of indigestion, which are usually quite brief. We may feel blown out or distended after a large meal and get some relief when we bring up wind. Most of the wind that we bring up is a result of swallowing air as we eat, but some is produced by a chemical reaction in the stomach or from carbonated, fizzy drinks. The solutions are to eat less, eat more slowly and go easy with fizzy drinks. You may have discovered for yourself that certain foods – fried onions, for example – give you an uncomfortable sensation in the upper abdomen, which lasts for only an hour or so. Again the answer is obvious: do not eat them.

More persistent indigestion is usually linked with the acid produced by the stomach. If the valve at the lower end of the oesophagus becomes weak or defective, the acid juices in the stomach may be pushed back upwards into the oesophagus causing a burning sensation (heartburn). This is often troublesome at night, when you lie flat. The underlying condition is called gastro-oesophageal reflux and is described in more detail starting on p.40.

Stomach acid may also cause problems if it attacks the lining of the stomach itself – peptic ulcer disease, described in detail starting on p.55. Our understanding of peptic ulcer disease has changed greatly in recent years, thanks to the discovery of an infective agent called *Helicobacter pylori* – you can find out more about this on p.56.

The third common type of indigestion, called non-ulcer dyspepsia, is something of a puzzle. This is the diagnosis given to people who have persistent symptoms of indigestion but in whom the tests for gastro-oesophageal reflux and stomach ulcers are normal. Dyspepsia is actually just the medical name for indigestion. Some people with this type of indigestion are eventually found to have a disorder affecting another part of the digestive system, such as gallstones or irritable bowel syndrome. In others, the pain is found to be caused by some disorders of the lower ribs and muscles of the abdominal wall. Most people with non-ulcer dyspepsia, however, seem to have sensitive stomachs, which cause symptoms at times of emotional stress. The condition is described in greater detail on p.74.

Rarely, indigestion may be the first symptom of a more serious condition such as stomach cancer. Stomach cancer is becoming less common than in the past, and it occurs much less frequently than peptic ulcer disease or gastro-oesophageal reflux. It is described in greater detail on p.79.

KEY POINTS

- During normal digestion, food is broken down so that it can be absorbed into the body.
- The stomach produces acid and pepsin to help in this process.
- If the lining of the stomach is weakened, or if acid production is altered, then a peptic ulcer may form.

Treating indigestion yourself

LOOK AFTER YOUR STOMACH
If you eat on the move, feeling tense and in a hurry, and you suffer from indigestion, a change in your lifestyle will probably reduce the symptoms.

Symptoms of indigestion are so common that we tend to think of them as something quite minor that we can treat ourselves with medicines bought over the counter at the chemist.

The range of remedies on offer is huge and they sell in great quantities. However, it is worth bearing in mind that symptoms mean that something is going wrong somewhere in the digestive system and, if you have anything more than the occasional mild attack, it is necessary to seek out and treat the cause rather than just dealing with the symptoms themselves. If simple self-help measures do not solve the problem, you should make an appointment to see your GP.

TAKING THE FIRST STEPS

Initially, however, if you have recently had one or two attacks of mild indigestion, it is worth trying to make some changes in your lifestyle so that you are being kinder to your stomach (see box opposite). It is important to improve your health in general.

Indigestion can be made worse or even be caused by treatment with medicines such as aspirin and other non-steroidal anti-inflammatory drugs taken for arthritis and

Lifestyle Changes

If you are experiencing occasional mild bouts of indigestion, there is a range of lifestyle changes that you can make to ease the problem.

- If you smoke you should stop.

- Try to lose weight and increase the amount of exercise you take – instead of taking the bus or driving you should walk or cycle.

- Do not drink too much alcohol. Men should not take more than 21 units of alcohol a week (one unit is equal to half a pint of beer or lager, a glass of wine or a measure of spirits ['short']). Women should not take more than 14 units of alcohol a week.

- Eat a healthier diet. Cut down on the amount of fatty food you eat, including fried food, butter, cheese, crisps and red meat. Instead, eat more fruit and grilled chicken or fish and try boiled potatoes instead of chips.

- Increase the amount of fibre in your diet. Fibre is found in fruit and vegetables and in high-fibre breakfast cereals and whole-grain bread.

- Avoid hot spices, salt and vinegar and certain salad foods (for example onions and tomatoes) as these often make heartburn worse.

- Decrease your caffeine intake by reducing the amount of tea and coffee you drink. Try decaffeinated coffee and, if you take fizzy drinks, try decaffeinated ones.

- Do not eat a large meal just before you go to bed; allow a few hours for your food to digest before lying down.

- Stomachs like routine and work better when you eat three or four meals at the same times each day.

- Anxiety and stress affect the way the stomach muscles work so try to take some time in the day to relax on your own for a short while.

Recognising a Unit of Alcohol

Alcohol is a common cause of indigestion, and reducing your intake will help. Various drinks contain different amounts of alcohol. A unit of alcohol contains approximately 8–10 grams of pure alcohol.

| Small glass of sherry = 1 unit | Small glass of wine = 1 unit | ½ pint of beer or cider, or ¼ pint of strong lager = 1 unit | Single measure of aperitif or spirit = 1 unit |

other painful disorders. These drugs reduce inflammation by decreasing the body's production of chemicals called prostaglandins. As well as causing inflammation in the joints, however, these chemicals also help the stomach protect itself against acid. This is why indigestion and ulcers are a common side-effect of these types of drugs. For more details on this, see p.63.

You may find that taking paracetamol, which does not irritate the stomach, instead of aspirin relieves your indigestion, but do not stop taking other anti-inflammatory drugs prescribed by your doctor without discussing this with him or her first.

ASKING THE PHARMACIST

Making changes to your lifestyle is not always sufficient to get rid of your indigestion but, if you have no worrying symptoms (see pp.25–27), it is reasonable to try treating your indigestion yourself for a couple of weeks. Making the right choice of over-the-counter medicine is not easy, and the best person to advise you is the pharmacist. He or she will be able to recommend the right type of medication for your particular symptoms and will also know whether it is safe to take it at the same time as any other prescription medicines that you may be on. Ask about cost before making up your mind too – for example, some heavily advertised medications may be more expensive than identical products sold by pharmacy chains under their own brand names.

What Kind of Pain?

The pharmacist will need to know your symptoms to give you the best advice.

- When do you get pain?
- What makes it worse?
- What makes it better?
- Have you lost weight recently?
- Do you have any other symptoms besides indigestion?
- What have you tried already?
- Are you or could you be pregnant?

To help the pharmacist to help you, you will need to explain your symptoms, be able to say when you get them and so on. The checklist in the above box may be useful in getting the relevant facts sorted out in your mind before you go to the pharmacy.

▬ OVER-THE-COUNTER REMEDIES ▬

There are several different types of indigestion remedy that you can buy over the counter without prescription.

ANTACIDS

These are simple alkalis that neutralise stomach acid for a short period. Examples of simple alkalis are aluminium hydroxide, magnesium trisilicate and sodium bicarbonate. Generally, they have no harmful effects, although some people do have problems with their side-effects on the bowels. Aluminium-containing antacids can cause

INDIGESTION REMEDIES
There is a wide range of indigestion remedies available over the counter, and your pharmacist will be able to advise you which to choose.

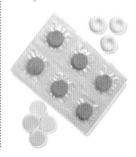

19

How Antacids Reduce Stomach Acid

Antacids are simple alkalis, taken by mouth in a tablet or liquid form, that neutralise the acid in the stomach for a short period. They have relatively few side-effects, but can worsen certain medical conditions.

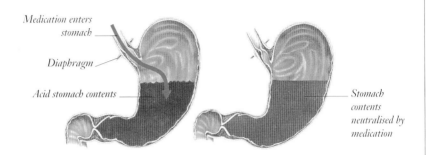

Medication enters stomach

Diaphragm

Acid stomach contents

Stomach contents neutralised by medication

constipation and magnesium-containing ones may cause diarrhoea. If you have other medical conditions, or are taking other prescribed medicines, you should discuss these with your pharmacist or your doctor before taking any of these over-the-counter medicines. This is especially important for anyone with heart disease, kidney disease or high blood pressure because many antacids contain salt (in the form of sodium bicarbonate), which can make these conditions worse. Some antacids (especially sodium bicarbonate) produce gas as they work, and this can cause belching. Dimethicone is a chemical that is often added to antacids to help reduce flatulence.

DRUGS THAT PROTECT

These drugs form a protective lining around the inside of the stomach and oesophagus, insulating against acid

How Drugs Protect the Stomach and Oesophagus

Drugs containing alginate are taken by mouth. They float on the top of the stomach contents, and if acid reflux occurs the alginate protects against acid damage by forming a protective lining around the oesophagus.

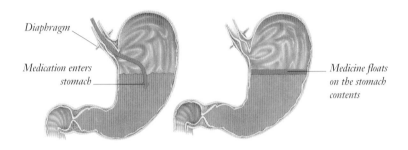

Diaphragm

Medication enters stomach

Medicine floats on the stomach contents

damage. They usually have several ingredients and often contain an antacid, but the main ingredient is alginate (made from seaweed). This floats on the stomach contents and, if gastro-oesophageal reflux occurs, the alginate soothes the lining of the oesophagus. Examples of alginate-containing drugs are Algicon, Gastrocote and Gaviscon. As these drugs all contain some antacid (some containing salt) you should talk to your doctor or pharmacist before using them if you have other medical conditions or if you take other medicines.

ANTISPASMODICS
These drugs act by reducing the tension in the muscle wall of the stomach. Some examples of antispasmodics are alverine citrate and peppermint oil. Peppermint-containing chewing gum has a similar effect. These drugs are most effective if you suffer from a 'nervous

NATURAL MEDICINES
Peppermint oil, derived from the peppermint plant, reduces tension in the muscle wall of the stomach and eases indigestion.

21

stomach' or trapped wind. These drugs, being natural products, have no important side-effects.

DRUGS THAT REDUCE STOMACH ACID

These drugs work by reducing the amount of acid produced by the stomach. They are very powerful and usually only available on prescription from your doctor.

Indigestion Remedies Available From Your Pharmacist

Examples of the main types of indigestion remedy available from the pharmacist are listed here, together with their actions, active ingredients and the proprietary names under which they are sold.

MEDICINE CLASS	ACTION	ACTIVE INGREDIENT	EXAMPLES
Antacids	Neutralise stomach acid	Magnesium trisilicate, aluminium hydroxide, sodium bicarbonate	Aludrox tablets, Rapeze, Rennie, Settlers tablets, soda mint tablets
Drugs that protect the stomach and oesophagus lining	Line the stomach and oesophagus preventing acid damage	Alginate	Algicon, Gastrocote, Gaviscon (these also contain antacid)
Antispasmodics	Reduce tension in the stomach wall muscles. Reduce bloatedness	Alverine, peppermint oil	Spasmonal, Colpermin, Mintec, peppermint chewing gum
H_2-receptor antagonists	Reduce stomach acid production	Cimetidine, famotidine, ranitidine	Tagamet, Pepcid, Boots Excess Acid Control, Zantac

They will be discussed in more detail later in the book. Some acid-suppressing drugs, known medically as H_2-receptor antagonists, are available over the counter, for example cimetidine, famotidine and ranitidine. The doses that you can buy are lower than those normally prescribed by a doctor, and they are only available in two-week packs. If your symptoms persist after two weeks of treatment you should see a doctor. H_2- receptor antagonists have been in use for many years now and several hundred million patients have taken them without side-effects. Nevertheless,a minority of people may develop side-effects when taking them, including drowsiness, headache, a rash and confusion (especially in elderly people). More importantly, cimetidine can affect the way that other medicines are processed by the liver (especially warfarin, used to thin the blood, phenytoin, used in the treatment of epilepsy, and aminophylline, used in the treatment of chronic asthma). You should not take cimetidine if you are also taking one of these other drugs.

The choice of over-the-counter remedies is vast and there is no real evidence that one is better than another. The best one is probably the one that you find most palatable and effective. They all taste different, and some trial and error may be required. The best time to take your antacid is usually before the time that you would normally expect your symptoms to occur – soon after meals and before bedtime – but again trial and error is often required. Many more powerful treatments are available on prescription only and they will be discussed in detail later starting on p.47.

KEY POINTS

- People who smoke get more indigestion than people who do not.

- A lot of indigestion is brought on by eating the 'wrong' food, such as fatty food.

- Often, improving the healthiness of your lifestyle will cure indigestion completely.

- A large number of indigestion remedies are available over the counter at the chemist.

- A pharmacist will be able to advise you which remedy is most suitable.

Do you need to see your doctor?

Probably three out of every four people who suffer from indigestion never seek medical advice: they relieve their symptoms by a few changes to their lifestyle and every now and then buy over-the-counter treatments, such as antacids or acid-blocking drugs, from the chemist.

Visiting Your Doctor
Your doctor will ask you detailed questions about any symptoms that you may be experiencing. He or she may be able to make a diagnosis on the basis of your answers, but, if there is any doubt as to the cause of your symptoms, you will be sent to hospital for further tests.

WHEN TO TAKE ACTION

One of the aims of this book is to help you to decide whether and when to consult your doctor. You should make an appointment if any of the three following descriptions applies to you.

SINISTER SYMPTOMS

See your GP without delay if you have any symptoms of the kind doctors call 'sinister', by which they mean symptoms that might be caused by a serious disease such as stomach cancer.

Early diagnosis and treatment give the best chance of a cure, so get prompt medical advice if you experience

any of the following symptoms:
- Unexplained weight loss.
- Loss of appetite.
- Difficulty swallowing.
- Vomiting blood or a brown material that bears a resemblance to ground coffee.
- Passing altered blood in the motions.
- Indigestion while you are taking non-steroidal anti-inflammatory drugs.

NO IMPROVEMENT

Although indigestion without these sinister symptoms can sensibly be treated at home in the first instance by changes to your lifestyle and over-the-counter remedies such as antacids, you should not persist if there is no improvement. Consult your doctor if your symptoms have not cleared up within two weeks of starting self-treatment.

Warning – Sinister Symptoms

Some symptoms may indicate a more serious disease, and you should consult your doctor if you develop any of the following:

- Weight loss.
- Poor appetite.
- Swallowing is difficult.
- Vomiting blood or material that looks like coffee grounds
- Blood in your stools (this will make your stools look 'tarry').
- Indigestion while you are taking non-steroidal anti-inflammatory drugs.

Unusual Symptoms

You should consult your doctor if you develop indigestion for the first time in your life after the age of 40, or if you develop a type of indigestion that you have not had before. Your doctor may need to arrange various tests and investigations before beginning treatment (see p.28).

What Your Doctor Will Do

If your indigestion does not clear up after two weeks with simple home treatment, it is sensible to ask your doctor's advice without further delay.

He or she will start off by asking a lot of questions about the exact symptoms you have been experiencing, how long they have been troubling you, what brings them on, what relieves them, and so on. This will usually be followed by a physical examination to identify any tender places in your abdomen and to check on your general health.

Your GP may be confident that he or she can deal with your problem straight away, or you may be referred to a hospital clinic for further tests. In fact, most people with indigestion do not need further tests. Your GP will usually be able to make an accurate diagnosis based entirely on your symptoms and then offer advice or treatment. If the symptoms suggest gastro-oesophageal reflux then advice about lifestyle with or without antacids will usually be all that you need. There are, however, three scenarios in which your doctor may feel that further investigation is warranted.

A Suspected Peptic Ulcer

Although your doctor may well be able to make a diagnosis based on your symptoms, this is not always the case. Some people who have 'typical' symptoms of a peptic ulcer turn out to have non-ulcer dyspepsia, and the treatment of the two conditions is entirely different. For this reason, if your doctor suspects a peptic ulcer then further tests are likely to be required. The most common test arranged is an endoscopy (see opposite), but your doctor might think that a test for infection with *Helicobacter pylori* is all that is required (see p.36).

FAILURE TO RESPOND

If you are one of the minority of people whose symptoms continue to be troublesome despite treatment, your doctor may arrange for you to have an endoscopy to make sure that you do not have some other condition that needs to be treated in a different way.

SINISTER SYMPTOMS

This term is used to describe symptoms that almost always indicate significant underlying disease and warrant further investigation. The most important are indigestion associated with loss of appetite and weight and difficulty swallowing. These symptoms always need urgent medical advice. Further investigations are also usually needed if your symptoms are of recent origin and you are over 40, unless the explanation is very obvious and straightforward. Stomach cancer is almost unheard of in those under 40 years of age, but it is always a possibility in people over this age who experience indigestion for the first time. Early diagnosis is essential if treatment is to be effective.

TESTS AND INVESTIGATIONS

Hospitals vary in the way that they organise tests requested by your GP: you may see one of the hospital doctors, or you may simply go for tests so that the results can then be sent to your own doctor, who will decide what needs to be done next. There are various tests that you might need, but they are likely to include one or more of the following:

• Routine blood tests: these are simply to check for common abnormalities such as anaemia. Your doctor may take the opportunity of a blood test to check for other common diseases unrelated to your stomach.

• Endoscopy (see below).

• Barium X-rays (see p.35).

• Tests for *Helicobacter pylori* infection (see p.36). This type of investigation is different from the previous two tests in that it is not looking for anything abnormal within the oesophagus or the stomach but for the actual cause of the problem.

ENDOSCOPY

An endoscope is an instrument that allows a doctor to look inside your body. There are endoscopes to examine the lungs and the windpipe, the lower bowel, the bladder and joints such as the knee, as well as the oesophagus, the stomach and the duodenum. This section is concerned with endoscopes used to look inside the oesophagus, the stomach and the duodenum. The early endoscopes used lenses and mirrors, but 30 years ago these were replaced by fibreoptic instruments that gave the operator a clear, direct view of the inside of the stomach. Modern endoscopes are very advanced bits of technology (and thus extraordinarily expensive), consisting of a flexible piece of tubing, the tip of which can be controlled by the operator. Older endoscopes have optical fibres along their length, but

ENDOSCOPE IMAGE
This image of the junction of the oesophagus with the stomach was taken using an endoscope, a flexible viewing instrument.

An Endoscopic Examination

An endoscope is a flexible viewing instrument that can be passed down the throat in order to look at the lining of the oesophagus, the stomach and the duodenum.

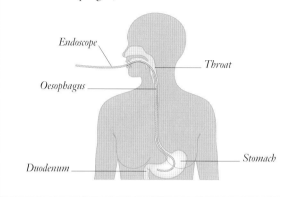

modern instruments actually have a small video camera in the tip and images are carried electronically direct to a video screen. The instrument also has other channels for suctioning stomach juice, blowing air to inflate the stomach and passing specialised forceps to take tiny biopsy specimens.

An endoscopy test (often called gastroscopy or simply the telescope test) is now the most accurate and most useful way of investigating the different causes of indigestion. It is the best way of diagnosing peptic ulcers and stomach cancers, and it can also be useful in diagnosing *Helicobacter pylori* infection. As well as giving the operator a clear view of any abnormalities, it also allows him or her to take tissue samples (biopsies) if necessary and can be used for treating other complications such as narrowing of the oesophagus.

HAVING AN ENDOSCOPY TEST

Depending on your symptoms, your GP may refer you to the hospital clinic for a full assessment or just for the endoscopy itself – a system known as 'fast track' or 'open access' endoscopy.

The procedure is usually carried out in a specialised unit within a hospital and takes only a few minutes. Endoscopy departments are extraordinarily busy places, however, and the check-in procedure before the test and booking out after the test may take an hour each. It is usually best to set aside the whole morning or afternoon depending on the time of your appointment. Your stomach needs to be empty for a complete test and so, for a morning test, you will be told to eat or drink nothing after your evening meal on the previous day, and for an afternoon test you should eat nothing after a light breakfast.

When you arrive at the department you will initially be directed to a waiting area with other patients and then to an area where you can be 'clerked in' by either a doctor or a nurse. The purpose of this is to explain the test and to answer your questions, but also to make sure that your general health is good enough for you to undergo the procedure, although it is very rare for anyone to be considered too ill. You will also be asked to sign a consent form. When it is your turn you will then be directed into the endoscopy room itself.

It is easy to be daunted by the numerous racks of equipment and machines in the endoscopy suite, but each has its own job to do and is individually straightforward. The most important pieces are the endoscope itself and its accompanying operating equipment, a video screen where the pictures appear and a machine that measures your pulse and oxygen levels using a clip on your finger.

This clever clip device works by shining a light through the soft tissue of your finger; changes in the amount of light absorbed show how 'red' your blood is and thus how much oxygen it is carrying.

As well as the endoscopist, there will also be a nurse to look after you and another member of staff to assist the endoscopist. You will be asked to lie down on your left side

Anaesthesia During an Endoscopy

Having an endoscope passed down your throat can cause some discomfort, so you may be offered a choice between two kinds of anaesthetic. You may prefer not to be anaesthetised.

What Are the Choices?

Some people feel that they will not be able to manage without some sedation, whereas others prefer to be wide awake and remain in control. The two anaesthetic options are a throat spray to numb your throat or a sedative injection that will relax you. Which option you choose depends on how you feel about the test. Both methods have advantages and disadvantages, and the final choice is usually left to the individual concerned, although different departments have different ways of working.

Throat Spray

This is the simplest option. Before inserting the endoscope, the endoscopist or assistant sprays some local anaesthetic solution onto the back of your throat, making it numb. You then lie comfortably on your side and remain wide awake throughout the test. The main advantage of having only the throat spray is that you remain in complete control throughout the procedure. Also, because you are not sedated, you may well be able to discuss the results of the test straightaway and be able to drive yourself home or back to work afterwards. The disadvantage of the throat spray is that, because there is no sedative effect, anyone who is very anxious may be unable to swallow the endoscope and complete the test. The throat spray affects swallowing for up to 30 minutes after use, and you will be made comfortable. You may be given a sedative or have some throat spray depending on which you prefer (see box opposite). The nurse will then place the monitoring clip on your finger and may give you some oxygen (usually with a sponge-tipped tube up your nose) before placing a small mouth guard between your teeth. This protects both your teeth from the endoscope and the

Anaesthesia During an Endoscopy (cont'd.)

so you are advised not to eat or drink until sensation has completely returned to normal to prevent food and liquids being inhaled or 'going down the wrong way'.

INTRAVENOUS SEDATION

This method is a little more time-consuming and requires the endoscopist to place a temporary needle in the back of your hand or arm before giving a sedative injection. It does not render you unconscious (unlike a general anaesthetic) but makes you feel much more relaxed and comfortable. You are still able to hear and to swallow when asked to do so. The main advantage of intravenous sedation is that it makes the test easier to cope with if you are anxious; you may not remember anything about it afterwards. The main disadvantages are that you may become disoriented and the effects of sedation take several hours to wear off completely. This means that you will need someone else to drive you home and you will not be able to return to work the same day. In fact, it is always a good idea to take someone with you when having an endoscopy, even if you plan to have throat spray rather than sedation, in case you change your mind at the last minute.

Another disadvantage of sedation is that you may not be able to get any results on the day of the test because of the effects on your memory. Endoscopy itself does not interfere with breathing in any way, but intravenous sedation can suppress breathing so it may not be suitable if you have heart or lung disease. Some departments also give throat spray to some patients who are being sedated.

endoscope from your teeth. When ready the endoscopist will place the tip of the endoscope over your tongue and into your throat. You will then be asked to swallow and, as you do so, the oesophagus will open up allowing the endoscope to pass down into your stomach. The nurse looking after you during the test will constantly remove saliva from your mouth with a sucker much like that used by dentists, and this helps to reduce the risk of you inhaling any fluid. You will be able to swallow with the tube in your throat, but fluid can collect in your mouth because the tube holds open the oesophagus, allowing liquid to reflux up from your stomach. Once the endoscope is in position, the test takes only a few minutes, during which time air is blown into the stomach so that a good view can be obtained. Depending on the findings, the endoscopist may take some biopsies (tissue samples), which are entirely painless. When the examination is complete the endoscope is withdrawn and you are taken back to the 'recovery' area.

During the test the main symptoms that you can expect are pressure within the throat and occasionally some tummy discomfort and belching because of the air that is introduced. As the endoscope is passed into your throat you may retch once or twice, which is a normal reaction and usually minor. Once you have completely recovered after the test you can go home.

IS ENDOSCOPY SAFE?

Endoscopy departments are very busy places and thus every member of staff that you meet will be an expert with a lot of experience. Endoscopy is an extremely safe procedure, and serious complications related to a simple diagnostic test are virtually unheard of. Very rarely, however, the oesophagus may tear as the endoscope is being inserted, but this complication usually only happens in patients who have previously undiagnosed abnormalities of the upper oesophagus. In any case, the risk is probably less than one per 10,000 procedures. Other less serious complications relate to intravenous sedation: if liquid is inhaled it may cause a chest infection, but this is very rare during a simple diagnostic test and is more likely to occur in frail and elderly people.

BARIUM X-RAYS

Barium X-rays are used nowadays far less than in the past because in most cases an endoscopy examination will give all the information needed. However, some GPs may not have access to a hospital department offering an endoscopy service and so may refer their patients for a barium X-ray instead. In any case, this may be a better option for some individuals, especially if the problem is in the oesophagus, as the test shows up the structure of the oesophagus and any muscle spasm will be visible.

Ordinary X-ray examinations of the kind used to assess broken bones give poor images of the internal organs. If, however, some barium sulphate is swallowed before the X-rays are taken it outlines the shape of the oesophagus and stomach. Barium is a heavy metal that is totally impenetrable by X-rays and so shows up on films and screens as opaque shadows. Barium sulphate is tasteless and causes no discomfort when you swallow it.

Barium X-ray examinations are generally carried out in the outpatient department, and you do not need an

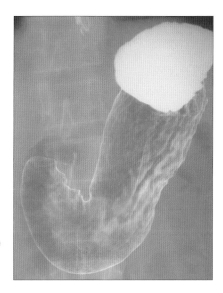

BARIUM X-RAY
This barium X-ray image shows a normal stomach. The barium has lined the wall of the stomach and collected in a mass at the top of the stomach because the patient is lying head down.

anaesthetic. The radiologist uses a fluorescent screen to watch the progress of the barium after you have swallowed it, and he or she will take pictures from time to time to provide a permanent record.

The whole examination usually takes about 20 to 30 minutes. The barium is eventually passed out in the faeces; it sometimes causes constipation, so you should eat a high-fibre diet for a day or two after the test has been done.

TESTS FOR *H. PYLORI*

If you are thought likely to be suffering from peptic ulcer disease, tests will be needed to determine whether your stomach is infected with *Helicobacter pylori* (*H. pylori*). This infection has an important role in causing ulcers, as explained on p.56. There are three ways of testing for *H. pylori* – examining a tissue sample from the stomach lining (a biopsy), a blood test and a breath test.

TISSUE TESTS

These require a tiny specimen of the stomach lining, called a biopsy, which is taken during an endoscopy. The specimen is placed in a special solution (either liquid or gel), which changes colour if *H. pylori* is present; this is called a urease test. *H. pylori* organisms secrete a protein chemical called urease, which converts urea (a substance present in the bloodstream and in urine produced by the breakdown of protein) to ammonia. The diagnostic solutions contain urea and an alkali indicator. If *H. pylori* is present within the biopsy placed in the test solution, then the urea is converted into ammonia, which causes the alkali indicator to change colour, thus producing a positive test. Depending on which test solution is used, the result takes from a few minutes to 24 hours to become available. In addition to the urease test, the biopsy specimen can also be sent to the pathology department to be looked at under the microscope. Not only can the microscopic *H. pylori* themselves be seen in this way, but so can the associated microscopic stomach inflammation called gastritis.

The main advantage of these tests is that they are the most accurate available and confirm whether or not active *H. pylori* is present at the time of the test. In addition, while performing the endoscopy, the doctor can see if there is any evidence of a peptic ulcer, suggesting that *H. pylori* should be eradicated.

The disadvantage of tissue testing is that it requires an endoscopy, but looking for *H. pylori* is rarely the only reason for doing such an investigation, so it makes sense to do a biopsy at the same time anyway. In common with some other *H. pylori* tests, the results can be incorrectly interpreted if you are taking a type of medication called a proton pump inhibitor (such as omeprazole, lanso-prazole or pantoprazole, see p.47), which suppresses the bacterium without actually killing it.

BREATH TEST

Like the tissue test, the urea breath test makes use of the fact that *H. pylori* secretes urease, which converts urea into ammonia, producing carbon dioxide as it does so. You are asked to eat nothing for 12 hours before a breath test and are then given a drink containing urea to which a tiny amount of perfectly safe radiation has been added. Thirty minutes later, a small breath sample is collected. If *H. pylori* is present in your stomach, the urea is converted into ammonia and carbon dioxide, which is then absorbed and excreted in your breath, along with a tiny amount of radioactivity. This can then be measured with a special machine in the hospital laboratory.

The advantage of the breath test is that it is very straightforward and takes a very short amount of time. Like the biopsy urease test, it is very accurate and confirms that you have active *H. pylori* infection present at the time of the test. This also means that, if necessary, the breath test can be performed repeatedly to check whether the bacteria have been eradicated after treatment. The disadvantage of the test, like some other *H. pylori* tests, is that the result may be inaccurate if you are taking proton pump inhibitor medication (see p.47). Also the result is not usually available for several days because of the measuring equipment used.

ANTIBODY BLOOD TEST

As with other infections, *H. pylori* infection triggers the production of specific antibodies in your blood. These can then be looked for with a simple blood test and the presence of these antibodies confirms *H. pylori* infection. Once your body has produced these antibodies they may persist for many years even after the infection has been eradicated.

For this reason, the blood test is useful for diagnosing infection only in a person who has never had *H. pylori* treatment, and it cannot be used more than once. The real advantage of the test is that it is very quick and is usually available in the GP's surgery. Unlike the other tests for *H. pylori*, the blood test is not influenced by any drugs that you may be taking.

KEY POINTS

- You should see your doctor if:
  - You have lost weight.
  - You have lost your appetite.
  - You have difficulty swallowing.
  - You vomit blood or material that looks like coffee grounds.
  - You have passed altered blood in the motions.
  - You have indigestion while taking anti-inflammatory drugs.
  - You are over 40 and have indigestion for the first time.
- Your doctor will ask about your symptoms and examine you.
- Often the cause of indigestion is straightforward and your doctor can offer you treatment immediately.
- If your doctor suspects a peptic ulcer or something more serious, then special tests will be arranged.
- The most usual test is to look into the stomach with a telescope – an endoscopy test.
- Other tests that are sometimes used are blood tests and barium X-rays.

Gastro-oesophageal reflux

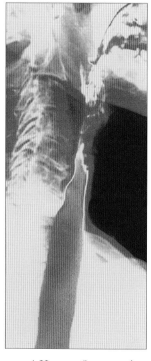

A HEALTHY SWALLOW
In this X-ray image, the patient is seen from the side, swallowing some barium. The healthy oesophagus (red) is narrowed as the muscles constrict to swallow.

Gastro-oesophageal reflux is the medical name for what most of us refer to as heartburn, although it can also cause other symptoms besides the burning pain in the centre of your chest.

It is the most common cause of indigestion and will affect most people at some stage in their lives. Usually the symptoms are relatively trivial, but they are often long-standing and can become quite disabling. The most common symptom produced by gastro-oesophageal reflux is the burning sensation that can radiate into the throat. It often comes and goes and can be brought on by certain foods, by stooping or by lying flat in bed at night. Sometimes gastro-oesophageal reflux is associated with difficulty swallowing or painful swallowing. Occasionally gastro-oesophageal reflux may cause regurgitation of food into the mouth and a feeling of nausea. Usually, a change in lifestyle is all that is required to ease symptoms, but there are also a number of useful antacid treatments available from the chemist (see p.19), and, for more severe cases, there are a number of highly effective drugs now available on prescription (see p.47).

It is important to point out at the outset that, in the vast majority of cases, gastro-oesophageal reflux is not serious and does not mean you have or are likely to develop another illness such as cancer. However, it is important to distinguish heartburn from another common cause of central chest pain, namely angina, especially in men or women over 50. Angina pain is usually brought on by exertion, such as brisk walking uphill, and is quickly relieved by rest, unlike reflux, so it is usually not difficult to tell one from the other. If you have pain that you think might be angina, you should consult your doctor without delay.

WHAT ARE THE CAUSES?

As explained earlier (see p.12), the glands in the stomach produce a cocktail of hydrochloric acid and pepsin (an enzyme) to aid in the initial breakdown

Action Checklist

Chest discomfort may be a sign that you have angina. You need to see your doctor without delay to investigate your symptoms if any of the following occur:

- You develop pain in the centre of your chest or upper abdomen for the first time.
- The pain changes in character or becomes more severe than usual.
- The pain is brought on by exercise and goes away when you rest.
- The pain radiates into your arms or neck.
- You experience other symptoms as well as pain, including sweating, nausea, shortness of breath, faintness, passing out or palpitations.

N.B. Burping or wind can be caused by angina as well as by heartburn so it is not in itself a clue to the correct diagnosis.

and subsequent digestion of food. In addition, this cocktail acts as an initial step in destroying any bacteria that are present in food. The stomach protects itself from the dangerous effects of the acid/pepsin mixture with a lining of special mucus. When the mixture leaves the stomach on its way into the intestine (the first part of which is called the duodenum), the acid is neutralised by alkaline juice from the pancreas.

The oesophagus is rather sensitive to acid, but in normal circumstances this is not important because the junction between the stomach and oesophagus is held tightly closed by a valve (the gastro-oesophageal valve), thus preventing any of the stomach contents from passing back up the oesophagus. Occasionally, however, the gastro-oesophageal valve is not completely tight and so allows acid and pepsin back up into the oesophagus, causing the symptoms outlined previously.

How Does Gastro-oesophageal Reflux Occur?

Gastro-oesophageal reflux occurs when the acidic stomach contents leak back into the oesophagus, causing the symptoms we know as heartburn. This happens when the valve at the top of the stomach fails to remain tightly closed.

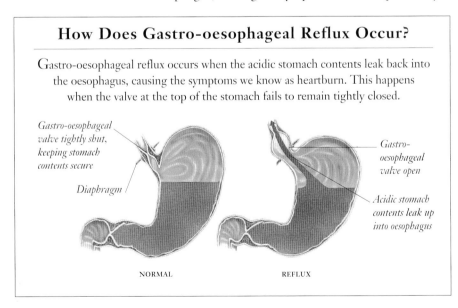

Gastro-oesophageal valve tightly shut, keeping stomach contents secure

Diaphragm

Gastro-oesophageal valve open

Acidic stomach contents leak up into oesophagus

NORMAL

REFLUX

The gastro-oesophageal valve has two components: the lower oesophageal sphincter muscle (the circular muscle fibres which squeeze the passage shut) and the slit-like opening in the diaphragm muscle through which the oesophagus passes (the diaphragm hiatus). Individually these two components are weak, but when working together they provide a tight junction. The function of this junction is very complex, and in the normal situation it is controlled by various reflexes. When we swallow, for example, the junction is required to relax at just the right time to allow food into the stomach, but when we are not swallowing the junction must remain tight to prevent gastro-oesophageal reflux.

PROBLEMS WITH THE VALVE

There are two main reasons why you may develop problems with your gastro-oesophageal valve. These may occur alone or together. The sphincter muscle at the bottom of the oesophagus may relax too much, or you may develop a fault where the oesophagus goes through the diaphragm – a hiatus hernia.

SPHINCTER MUSCLE PROBLEMS

In some people there may be no obvious explanation why this muscle does not function as it should, but factors that are known to play a part are: being overweight, heavy alcohol consumption, smoking, certain foodstuffs (fatty foods, onions, spicy foods, chocolate and acidic foods) and occasionally prescribed

Lifestyle Factors

A number of lifestyle factors are known to play a role in causing stomach sphincter muscle problems. These include:

- Being overweight
- Drinking excess alcohol
- Smoking
- Too much fat in the diet, or eating spicy or acidic foods
- Some prescription drugs

drugs. All of these are more likely to cause problems near bedtime, so that you are at increased risk of reflux when you lie down.

H I A T U S   H E R N I A

Sometimes, the hiatus (opening) in the diaphragm is too large, allowing the upper part of the stomach to slip above the diaphragm. The result is that the two parts of the gastro-oesophageal valve are no longer aligned, thus reducing its strength and allowing reflux of acid into the oesophagus. Having a hiatus hernia does not always cause symptoms – in fact most people do not get any. What hiatus hernias do is make gastro-oesophageal reflux more likely and this is what causes the symptoms. No one knows why a hiatus hernia may develop, but they are known to be extremely common (especially in those aged over 65 years) and often they go undetected, causing no trouble throughout a person's whole life.

C O N S E Q U E N C E S   O F   R E F L U X

In most people reflux of acid and pepsin into the oesophagus causes symptoms but does no actual damage. In a small proportion of people, however, there is damage to the lining of the oesophagus in the form of inflammation known as oesophagitis.

O E S O P H A G I T I S

Although no one knows why some people with reflux get oesophagitis and others do not, it is thought to be more likely to develop in tobacco smokers. With appropriate treatment oesophagitis can be healed but, if you have had it for a long time, there are two more serious conse-quences: oesophageal strictures and Barrett's oesophagus.

OESOPHAGEAL STRICTURES

Long-standing inflammation of the oesophagus can lead to scar formation which, in turn, can lead to narrowing of the oesophagus making swallowing difficult. This will require specialist treatment in hospital. The treatment of oesophageal strictures is discussed on p.52. It is important to emphasise that difficulty swallowing always requires full evaluation by a doctor as soon as possible and often requires hospital treatment.

BARRETT'S OESOPHAGUS

After many years of exposure to acid, the lining of the oesophagus slowly changes to resemble that of the stomach (with its self-protecting mucus). This condition is named Barrett's oesophagus after the doctor who first discovered it. In many cases there are no adverse consequences, but it is known to be one of the causes of oesophageal cancer; for this reason, you will probably need to be followed up closely in hospital if the condition is extensive.

HOW IS IT DIAGNOSED?

Your doctor will normally be able to diagnose gastro-oesophageal reflux from your symptoms without needing to refer you for tests, especially if, like many people, you have been getting the same symptoms for years. On the other hand, tests may be needed to confirm the diagnosis or to make sure you do not have some other condition requiring different treatment if:

- You are over 40 and your symptoms change.
- You are over 40 and have symptoms for the first time.
- You have any difficulty swallowing.
- Your symptoms do not respond to treatment.

The most commonly used and most useful test in this context is the upper gastrointestinal endoscopy (see p.29). A barium X-ray (see p.35) may sometimes be helpful as it will show up any muscle spasm. In those relatively rare cases where the diagnosis is still not clear from the results of these tests, there are other possible kinds of hospital investigation. These include measuring the amount of acid that is in the oesophagus and measuring the pressure in the oesophagus using special probes passed via the nose.

TREATING REFLUX

Treatment of reflux, as with any medical condition, is based first on elimination of the underlying causes. It is most important to change any aspects of your lifestyle which may be making the condition worse, as explained earlier (see p.43):

- If you smoke, make up your mind to stop and do it. Smoking makes heartburn more likely and is bad for your general health.
- Lose weight if necessary – try to take regular exercise as well as making any necessary changes to your diet.
- Keep your alcohol intake to a minimum or cut it out altogether.
- Avoid eating any foods that you know trigger your symptoms. Do not overfill your stomach but rather eat little and often. Always sit down to eat and make a point of eating slowly and chewing your food well.
- Do not wear tight belts or underclothes.
- Do not eat or drink just before going to bed.
- Prop the head end of the bed up by about six inches so that you sleep on a gentle incline – putting telephone directories under the back legs works well. You may

also find it helpful to sleep on your left side.

• Avoid bending at the waist or stooping immediately after you have eaten.

Making these changes is all that is necessary for many people, but they do not work for everyone. Even so, if your symptoms improve sufficiently so that they trouble you much less than before, you may not need any further treatment.

MEDICAL TREATMENT

Many of the medications available over the counter, such as antacids and the H_2-receptor blockers (see p.22), may be all that is needed to control your symptoms, although your doctor can prescribe more powerful drugs if necessary. These fall broadly into two categories: proton pump inhibitors and prokinetic drugs. These medicines are available on prescription from your doctor.

PROTON PUMP INHIBITORS

These are a group of acid-suppressing drugs that have been developed relatively recently, including, for example, omeprazole, lansoprazole and pantoprazole. These are extremely powerful drugs and can be used to treat gastro-oesophageal reflux if your symptoms have not responded to more simple measures. They suppress stomach acid only while you are actually taking them, so your symptoms of reflux will come back if you stop. This means that you may have to take them on a long-term basis, rather than as a single 'course' of treatment, in which case side-effects become important.

The fact that these drugs are relatively new means that doctors are still building up knowledge about them.

Proton Pump Inhibitors

These drugs work by preventing the acid-producing cells in the stomach lining from functioning in the normal way, thereby reducing the amount of acid present in the stomach. They need to be taken on a long-term basis.

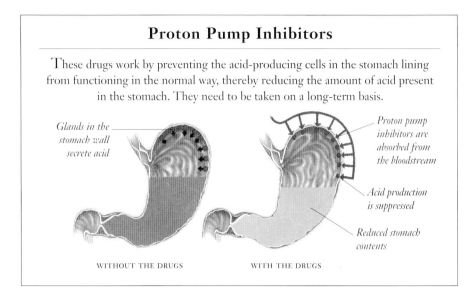

Glands in the stomach wall secrete acid

Proton pump inhibitors are absorbed from the bloodstream

Acid production is suppressed

Reduced stomach contents

WITHOUT THE DRUGS   WITH THE DRUGS

They may cause minor side-effects, similar to those of the H_2-receptor antagonists, such as drowsiness, headache, rash and possibly confusion in older people. However, because proton pump inhibitors are so powerful, they reduce the stomach acid to almost zero. This has two important side-effects. One of the functions of stomach acid, as mentioned previously, is that it helps to kill any bacteria present in food that you have eaten. Thus, the most common consequence of absence of stomach acid is an increased risk of gastroenteritis. In a normal healthy individual, this is not usually a problem (unless they travel abroad when travellers' diarrhoea may be more common), but very elderly or infirm people may develop severe gastroenteritis. The second concern about taking proton pump inhibitors long term is that they have been shown to thin the lining of the stomach (a condition known medically as gastric atrophy). Whether this atrophy in individuals taking the drugs long term will turn out to be important is not known, but it is a matter of intense debate among doctors. Currently, proton pump inhibitors are thought to be safe to take long term, although this advice may change in the future. A sensible approach is only to take them long term if absolutely necessary.

PROKINETIC DRUGS

The name 'prokinetic' actually means 'helping movement'. These drugs help the muscles of the stomach wall become more effective at preventing gastro-oesophageal reflux and encourage the stomach to empty more efficiently. In addition, they tighten up the valve at the top of the stomach, which helps to prevent reflux.

Both these effects are achieved through the drugs' action on the nerve endings that control the muscles in

Prokinetic Drugs

These drugs do not prevent acid production. Instead they work by helping the muscles of the stomach wall to function more effectively, reducing the likelihood of reflux and helping the stomach to empty more efficiently.

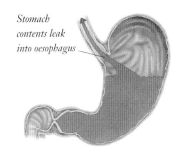

Stomach contents leak into oesophagus

WITHOUT THE DRUGS

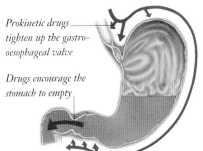

Prokinetic drugs tighten up the gastro-oesophageal valve

Drugs encourage the stomach to empty

WITH THE DRUGS

the stomach. As well as playing a role in the treatment of reflux, prokinetic drugs are especially useful for people with an 'anxious' stomach and are sometimes prescribed for non-ulcer dyspepsia (see p.74), with or without other treatments.

These drugs are usually taken regularly throughout the day and, as with acid-suppressing drugs, they may need to be taken long term. Examples of prokinetic drugs are metoclopramide, domperidone and cisapride. Generally these drugs are safe but, because of their prokinetic effects on the intestine, they can cause crampy tummy pain and diarrhoea. Metoclopramide is not usually given to young women or children because it can cause severe muscle spasms in the face and neck (called a dystonic reaction). This side-effect is much less common in men and older women.

SURGERY

Before the advent of potent acid-suppressing drugs, severe gastro-oesophageal reflux was frequently treated by means of surgery.

Briefly, the operation has two parts. First, the surgeon performs an operation to make the hole in the diaphragm smaller with some stitches, thereby correcting any hiatus hernia. Second, he or she tightens the lower oesophageal sphincter using part of the stomach wrapped around itself as a belt.

Originally this operation was a major undertaking requiring several days in hospital and many weeks off work, but now it is usually done as a 'keyhole' procedure and is much less disabling. This is because, instead of working through a large incision, the surgeon operates using endoscopes with the help of video cameras, and he or she only needs to make very small cuts through which the instruments are inserted. The result is that the recovery time after surgery is much shorter. However, the operation may be technically more difficult to perform, especially if the patient is overweight.

With the advent of less arduous operations, and because treatment for gastro-oesophageal reflux may need to be continued over a long period, anti-reflux surgery is once again becoming more popular. However, any operation does carry risks, and about 15 per cent of people will have some symptoms afterwards (in particular an inability to belch or vomit), so surgery is usually reserved for those individuals who do not respond to, or who cannot take, medical treatment for one reason or another. If surgery is to be considered the surgeon is likely to arrange further tests before going ahead, so as to be sure that you would benefit from having surgery done.

REFLUX COMPLICATIONS

Complications of gastro-oesophageal reflux usually only affect people who have severe symptoms that have not received treatment, especially elderly people, but they can also be the first sign of the condition. Such complications can only be diagnosed by endoscopy (with or without a biopsy) and/or barium X-ray.

TREATMENT OF COMPLICATIONS

Oesophagitis can be treated in a similar way to gastro-oesophageal reflux itself. However, the treatment for both oesophageal strictures and Barrett's oesophagus is less straightforward.

OESOPHAGITIS

Treatment for oesophagitis is very similar to that for uncomplicated gastro-oesophageal reflux, although for the initial few weeks a proton pump inhibitor (see p.47) is likely to be recommended to ensure that the oesophagitis heals. Once the oesophagitis has healed, patients are usually given the simplest and least powerful (and therefore least dangerous) treatment that is effective at controlling symptoms long term. In addition to dietary modification and weight loss, occasional simple antacids may be all that is needed. Some patients, however, require more powerful treatment on prescription from their doctor long term, such as H_2-receptor antagonists or even proton pump inhibitors.

OESOPHAGEAL STRICTURES

Scarring and narrowing of the oesophagus, caused by long-standing oesophagitis, may respond to treatment with proton pump inhibitors alone, but if you have any significant difficulty with swallowing other treatment may also be necessary. If your oesophagus has become narrowed, it can be stretched during an endoscopy procedure with relative safety, although the problem may recur. The procedure may be done either by passing dilators of gradually increasing size through the oesophagus or by inserting a catheter with a deflated balloon into the oesophagus, then inflating the balloon. This stretches the narrowed area and the catheter and balloon can then be removed. Most doctors recommend that anyone who has had an oesophageal stricture because of reflux should take proton pump inhibitors on a long-term basis (often for the rest of their lives) to help prevent its recurrence. Even with these drugs, narrowing can recur, but it usually responds to repeated stretching during a further endoscopy test. Again it is worth stressing that difficulty swallowing is always important and means that you should see your doctor without delay.

BARRETT'S OESOPHAGUS

There is at present no proven effective treatment for Barrett's oesophagus, although in the future there may be a role for laser treatment down an endoscope. Fortunately, the fact that you have this condition is not likely to interfere with your quality of life or life expectancy. However, it is known that, over a period of many years, Barrett's oesophagus may develop into an oesophageal cancer; so, if your condition is severe and you are young and otherwise fit, you are likely to be enrolled in an annual screening programme. This involves having annual endoscopies to look for signs that a cancer may be about to develop. If such signs are found, then the only way to prevent cancer developing for certain is an operation to remove the oesophagus, which is an extremely major undertaking. It is for this reason that only those patients fit enough for such an operation are usually offered screening. Depending on how much of the oesophagus needs to be removed, it may be necessary to raise the stomach up higher or to substitute a piece of colon for the part of the oesophagus that is taken out. Barrett's oesophagus itself does not cause symptoms, but if you have it you may well need long-term treatment with proton pump inhibitors for severe symptoms caused by gastro-oesophageal reflux.

KEY POINTS

- Heartburn is caused by reflux of stomach acid into the bottom of the oesophagus, possibly as a result of a hiatus hernia.

- Drug treatment is aimed at decreasing stomach acidity if lifestyle measures are not effective.

- In severe cases, reflux can damage the lower end of the oesophagus, necessitating hospital treatment.

Peptic ulcers and *Helicobacter pylori*

Peptic ulcers are another major cause of indigestion, although less common than gastro-oesophageal reflux. Peptic ulcers can occur anywhere in the upper intestinal tract but they are usually found in the stomach or in the first few inches of the upper intestine, the duodenum.

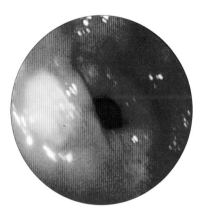

GASTRIC ULCER
This endoscope image shows a gastric ulcer. A small area of the lining of the stomach has been disrupted by acid, pepsin and bile, creating an indentation or sore.

Medically speaking, an ulcer is a small area of tissue that has lost its upper layers, so that an indentation or sore is created. Peptic ulcers are similar in form to mouth ulcers but tend to be deeper and so do not heal as quickly. The 'peptic' part of the name is derived from pepsin, the enzyme that helps break down food, but peptic ulcer disease covers both gastric (stomach) and duodenal ulcers.

SYMPTOMS

The predominant symptom caused by peptic ulcers is pain in the central upper abdomen. It is often described as a burning pain and can occur at any time, although often it is related to meal times. The symptoms of an ulcer in the stomach or in the duodenum can be identical, but often a duodenal ulcer

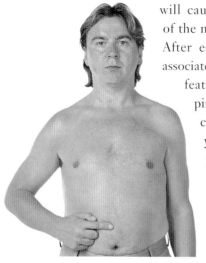

will cause pain, particularly in the early hours of the morning, that is relieved by a milky drink. After eating, a stomach ulcer may cause pain associated with a feeling of nausea. One particular feature of the pain is that you can usually pinpoint it very accurately, whereas in other conditions pain tends to be more diffuse. If you have a peptic ulcer your symptoms probably come and go – you may have good periods lasting a few weeks, interspersed with bad periods when you get pain every day. You may well have had symptoms of indigestion on and off for many years.

STOMACH ULCER PAIN
One of the features of a stomach ulcer is that the pain can be pinpointed very accurately.

CAUSES

As mentioned previously, the stomach glands produce a cocktail of acid and pepsin that acts to help digestion of food. The stomach and duodenum protect themselves from acid damage by secreting a layer of protective mucus. It is when the balance between attack and defence breaks down that a peptic ulcer may develop. There are a number of reasons why this may occur, but the most common cause is a bacterium, the discovery of which has transformed peptic ulcer management.

THE *HELICOBACTER* STORY

Before the early 1980s peptic ulcers were thought to be caused largely by an individual's lifestyle, although it was acknowledged that other factors might be involved. Peptic ulcers were known to be more common in tobacco smokers and also in those from socially disadvantaged backgrounds. In addition 'stress' was thought to be important, and both patients and doctors often attributed an ulcer to a stressful lifestyle. With the advent of powerful acid-suppressing drugs, H_2-receptor antagonists in the late 1960s and proton pump inhibitors in the late 1970s, ulcers could often be healed without the need for surgery, but it was not uncommon for them to recur after treatment, presumably for the same reasons that the ulcer began in the first place.

In the early 1980s two doctors in Australia, Warren and Marshall, working on specimens of stomach tissue, discovered a bacterium living in the mucus lining of the lower half of the stomach. The precise role of this bacterium, which they named *Campylobacter pylori*, was unclear. In general, the stomach is sterile, but this bacterium had found a way of concealing itself in the mucus lining where it could not be attacked and destroyed like other bacteria. Warren and Marshall discovered that, when the infection was present in the stomach, it was always associated with some microscopic inflammation of the lining called gastritis. At first it was not known whether the infection caused the gastritis or whether the gastritis allowed the infection to occur. To resolve this issue, Dr Marshall infected himself with the bacterium and tests showed that he did indeed develop gastritis, which disappeared after he successfully eradicated the infection with antibiotics. This proved that it was the infection that caused the gastritis. More recently the scientific name of the bacterium has been changed to *Helicobacter pylori* (*H. pylori*) and it has been discovered

HELICOBACTER PYLORI Discovered in the 1980s, this bacterium lives in the mucus lining of the stomach and can cause gastritis in some people.

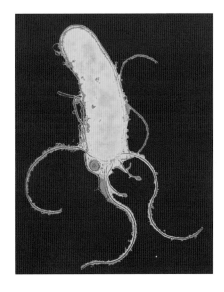

that a large proportion of the population, possibly as many as 40 per cent, have the infection in their stomachs. Most have no symptoms, but it is now known that a proportion of people – probably around 10 per cent of those infected – will go on to develop a peptic ulcer. Studies on several thousands of patients with duodenal or gastric ulcers have shown that the vast majority have *H. pylori* infection of the lower stomach and, more importantly, that eradication of the infection with a one-week course of medication results in long-term cure of the ulcer.

How Do You Become Infected?

Helicobacter pylori infection is usually acquired early in life from other members of the family. It can be passed on by close contact and is more common in large families sharing a small house. You are also more likely to pick up the infection in situations where lots of young adults share a confined space, such as in an army barracks. Exactly how it is transmitted is not known, but *H. pylori* has been shown to be present in saliva and probably in faeces as well. In most circumstances it is probably impossible to prevent spread of the infection but, as with other intestinal infections, good personal hygiene is important. As mentioned above, *H. pylori* infection is present in 40 per cent of the entire population. It is known to be more common in those over the age of 65, which may be because the infection was spread more easily under the conditions of the Second World War.

The Consequences of Infection

Most people infected with *Helicobacter pylori* will suffer no symptoms from it for their entire lives. In a proportion (probably in the region of 10 per cent),

The Formation of an Ulcer

An ulcer occurs when the mucus layer that protects the stomach and duodenum breaks down and allows acids and enzymes to erode the underlying tissues.

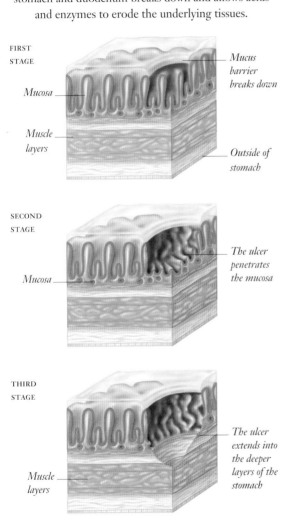

FIRST STAGE

Mucosa

Muscle layers

Mucus barrier breaks down

Outside of stomach

SECOND STAGE

Mucosa

The ulcer penetrates the mucosa

THIRD STAGE

Muscle layers

The ulcer extends into the deeper layers of the stomach

however, a peptic ulcer will develop. It is not known why some people develop ulcers whereas others do not, but it probably relates to the age at which the infection was acquired and to the particular type of *H. pylori* with which the person is infected. The mechanism of ulcer formation is complicated but is probably two-fold. *H. pylori* infection in the lower stomach 'fools' the stomach into producing more acid. It also causes thinning of the lining of the stomach, allowing acid to penetrate. Peptic ulcers caused by *H. pylori* infection are otherwise identical to those resulting from other causes, so special tests are usually undertaken to diagnose infection in anyone with a peptic ulcer.

H. pylori infection without a peptic ulcer is not thought to cause any symptoms, although it may play a part in some cases of what is called 'non-ulcer dyspepsia' (see p.74). In particular *H. pylori* infection does not cause heartburn and gastro-oesophageal reflux. Indeed it is thought that infection may in some way protect against some of the symptoms of reflux and, when *H. pylori* infection is eradicated from people who already have gastro-oesophageal reflux, their symptoms may actually get worse. This is because, in patients with gastro-oesophageal reflux, those with *H. pylori* infection benefit from a stomach acid-neutralising effect, similar to that of antacids, caused by *H. pylori*. This is different to the effect that *H. pylori* has in patients with a duodenal ulcer, where acid is increased. The reason for these differences is not yet completely understood.

The most controversial area of debate about *H. pylori* infection is whether it can cause stomach cancer. Certainly, the infection has not been proved to cause stomach cancer and, more importantly, eradication of the infection has not been shown to reduce the risk of stomach cancer. Eradication of *H. pylori* infection once a stomach cancer has developed has absolutely no effect, but it is certainly effective, and may lead to a complete cure, in patients who have a very rare condition known as lymphoma of the stomach (a tumour of the stomach's blood cells).

WHO NEEDS TREATMENT?

The decision as to whether an individual infected with *H. pylori* needs to be treated in order to eradicate the bacteria will be made on the basis of recommendations from the British Society of Gastroenterology and the National Institutes of Health in the USA (see box below).

Recommendations for Treatment

The British Society of Gastroenterology and the USA National Institutes of Health have guidelines to help doctors decide whether an individual infected with H. pylori needs eradication treatment.

- If you currently have a peptic ulcer, getting rid of H. pylori allows it to heal.

- If you have had a peptic ulcer in the past, which was not treated by surgery, eradication of H. pylori prevents the ulcer recurring.

- If you do not have and have not previously had a peptic ulcer, eradication is not necessary if you have gastro-oesophageal reflux, and it may make symptoms worse.

- Eradication of H. pylori is not currently recommended in patients with non-ulcer dyspepsia, although this issue is in debate.

- Eradication is not currently thought to be beneficial in preventing stomach cancer, although it is recommended for anyone who has the very rare stomach lymphoma.

- Unless you are in one of the groups of people for whom eradication is thought to be beneficial, you will not need to be tested for H. pylori infection.

HOW IS THE INFECTION ERADICATED?

Helicobacter pylori, unlike most common infections, is quite difficult to eradicate, and you need to take several different drugs at the same time. The reason for this is that the infection resides in a very sheltered environment within the stomach mucus layer and is protected from most drugs. Having said that, over the last 10 years numerous different drug regimens have been developed that, if taken correctly, get rid of the infection in 90 per cent of people who take them. The most common regimens all consist of three drugs taken together for a period of seven days. Two of the drugs are antibiotics and the third is a powerful acid-suppressing drug, usually omeprazole or lansoprazole. Modern regimens are very safe and cause few problems to those taking them, but some of the antibiotics can cause nausea and vomiting or diarrhoea (which can be serious in elderly people), and they must not be taken with alcohol. It is important to complete the course as prescribed, if possible, because the most common reason why treatment is unsuccessful is that people do not take it properly.

After a course of treatment to eradicate *H. pylori* infection it is important to check that it has worked by means of one of the *H. pylori* tests described previously (see p.36), usually a urea breath test. Around one in ten people may need a second course of treatment because the first one has been unsuccessful. Occasionally, even several courses of treatment fail to eradicate the bacterium and, in this situation, further attempts are usually abandoned in favour of different treatment. It is very unusual for people to become re-infected with the bacterium once it has been successfully eradicated.

If the symptoms persist after the successful eradication of *H. pylori*, it must be because the symptoms are the result of something else.

THE FUTURE OF *H. PYLORI*

Helicobacter pylori has probably been present in mammals for several thousands of years, and in most it seems to cause no ill effects. Although infection undoubtedly causes disease in a few, it may actually have benefits, as yet undiscovered, for the remainder who are infected. This is an area of intense debate among doctors and is one of the reasons why eradication of infection is not recommended routinely for people who do not have ulcers. It is possible that, in the future, scientists and doctors may discover different 'bad' *H. pylori* and 'good' *H. pylori* and so be able to target only the 'bad' ones for eradication. Along the same lines, it is possible that a vaccine could then be developed against 'bad' *H. pylori* and be given to babies, so preventing them acquiring the infection in the first place and thereby practically eradicating peptic ulcer disease.

ALTERNATIVE CAUSES

The other main cause of peptic ulcers is non-steroidal anti-inflammatory drugs, although very rarely other conditions may cause peptic ulcers.

ANTI-ARTHRITIS DRUGS

Non-steroidal anti-inflammatory drugs (often called simply NSAIDs) are used for treatment of arthritis and muscular aches and pains (these include aspirin, indomethacin, ibuprofen, diclofenac and naproxen). Some of these are also used to relieve headaches and period pains, and ibuprofen (sold over the counter under brand

ANTI-ARTHRITIS DRUGS
Patients taking NSAIDs to treat arthritis can develop a peptic ulcer as a result of the drugs. Treatment may have to be stopped or replaced with a potentially safer NSAID.

names such as Nurofen and Advil) is also found in many cold and 'flu remedies. If taken regularly over a long period (to treat rheumatoid arthritis, for example), these drugs may cause ulcers by interfering with the defence system of the duodenum and stomach. Using them occasionally rarely has the same effect but may make your symptoms worse if you already have an ulcer.

The drugs exert their anti-inflammatory effect within the body by reducing the production of chemicals called prostaglandins. If you injure yourself or get an infected cut, the damaged area becomes hot, red and painful. This is the result of prostaglandins, chemicals released from damaged cells around the injury. In most parts of the body where prostaglandins make inflammation worse (for example, inside the joints of people with arthritic conditions), NSAIDs are very effective. In the stomach, however, prostaglandins are a very important part of the mucus layer defence system and general, widely acting NSAIDs decrease these prostaglandins, weakening this defence and allowing peptic ulcers to develop in some people.

Newer NSAIDs (that are known as cyclo-oxygenase 2 inhibitors) are being developed (for example, meloxicam). These reduce prostaglandin production in the rest of the body without affecting production in the stomach. In the future, these drugs may help to reduce the number of peptic ulcers caused by use of anti-inflammatory drugs. It is important to point out that, although NSAIDs do not cause ulcers in most people who are taking them, you should always consult your doctor if you get indigestion while taking them.

LESS COMMON CAUSES

Peptic ulcers very occasionally occur in people who do not have *Helicobacter pylori* infection and who are not on NSAIDs. These ulcers, although they usually respond well to treatment, often remain unexplained. Very rarely peptic ulcers may be caused by other conditions usually diagnosed only in hospital. Examples are Crohn's disease (a condition that can affect any part of the intestine), Zollinger–Ellison syndrome (named after the doctors who first discovered it, this is a condition in which the stomach produces too much acid as a result of a hormone imbalance) and lymphoma (a tumour of the blood cells within the stomach wall).

Although smoking itself is no longer thought to be an independent cause of peptic ulcers, it is known that tobacco smoking significantly impairs ulcer healing, so anyone who has an ulcer and smokes is advised to stop.

COMPLICATIONS

In most cases, peptic ulcers cause rather unpleasant symptoms but nothing more serious. There are, however, three potentially more serious complications: bleeding, perforation and pyloric stenosis. Although it is also the case that people with stomach cancer are sometimes found to have a gastric ulcer, there is no real evidence that 'ordinary', benign stomach ulcers can become cancerous.

BLEEDING

Occasionally a peptic ulcer can 'burrow' into one of the arteries of the stomach or duodenum wall and cause bleeding. This can be very severe and blood may then be vomited up or pass through the intestine and appear in the motions. Vomit that contains old blood actually looks like coffee grounds because of the way the blood changes its appearance after being in contact with stomach acid. Similarly, once blood has travelled through the intestine it appears jet black and tarry. This is always important and, whether you have indigestion or not, you should always see your doctor straight away after vomiting blood or passing jet-black tarry motions.

PERFORATION

Occasionally, a peptic ulcer may erode completely through the stomach or duodenum wall so that acid gets into the abdominal cavity, causing peritonitis. If there is any leakage of stomach contents into the abdomen, the person experiences severe pain and infection may develop. This usually happens out of the blue to someone who has been suffering from indigestion and, as it can be fatal without treatment, emergency surgery will be needed immediately to repair the hole.

PYLORIC STENOSIS

This is the medical name for a condition in which the pylorus – the valve at the bottom of the stomach – becomes narrowed and so does not work properly. Repeated ulceration, over a period of several months or years, at the junction between the stomach and duodenum, can cause a severe scar that is so tight that it does not allow food and liquid to leave the stomach. Unlike ordinary tissue, an area that is scarred is not flexible and has a tendency to shrink over time. Sometimes, pyloric stenosis may be caused by swelling around an ulcer, but the swelling will subside if the person is given acid-suppressing drug treatment. The condition may develop in someone who has had indigestion on and off for years, and the main symptoms are recurrent vomiting and a feeling of fullness. It can usually be successfully treated with drugs, but occasionally an operation to enlarge the opening may be necessary if the narrowing is very severe.

STOMACH CANCER

Very occasionally, a person with a stomach ulcer (though not a duodenal ulcer) may be found to have stomach cancer (see p.79). For this reason, whenever a stomach ulcer is diagnosed specimens are usually taken from it to be examined under the microscope for evidence of cancer cells. If you have a stomach ulcer, you will normally be followed up closely with regular hospital checks to make sure that your ulcer is healing with treatment. Treatment is otherwise similar to that for duodenal ulcers – that is, antibiotics and acid-suppressing drugs (see p.69).

KEY POINTS

- If your doctor suspects a peptic ulcer, further tests of your stomach will be arranged.

- Peptic ulcers occur when the mucus lining of the stomach is damaged by acid.

- The most common cause of peptic ulcer is an infection of the stomach by a bacterium called *Helicobacter pylori*.

- The infection is common, affecting four out of ten people; for reasons that are not understood, only a minority of people with the infection ever develop a peptic ulcer.

- Peptic ulcers caused by *Helicobacter* can usually be healed with a course of antibiotics to cure the infection.

- Nowadays, surgery is only rarely required to treat complicated ulcers.

- *Helicobacter* infection by itself, without a peptic ulcer, is only treated in special circumstances.

- Anti-inflammatory drugs and aspirin can cause peptic ulcers by damaging the stomach's lining.

- If you develop indigestion while taking one of these treatments, you should consult your doctor.

Treating a peptic ulcer

Even though your doctor may be fairly certain from your symptoms that you have a peptic ulcer, he or she will usually arrange for you to have further tests to confirm the diagnosis.

The most reliable of those tests currently available is the upper gastrointestinal endoscopy, often known simply as endoscopy. This has largely replaced barium X-ray tests (although these are still occasionally required). *Helicobacter pylori* (*H. pylori*) infection can also be diagnosed at the time of an endoscopy test (in addition to other means). For details of these tests, see p.28 onwards.

PEPTIC ULCER
Your doctor should be able to tell from your symptoms if you have a peptic ulcer, but you will probably have further tests to confirm the diagnosis.

FORMS OF TREATMENT

Treatment of peptic ulcers has been revolutionised over the last decade or so by the advent of newer ulcer-healing drugs, in addition to the discovery that eradication of *H. pylori* infection is often all that is required. Although lifestyle changes such as giving up smoking are important and will be helpful, they are unlikely to be successful alone (unlike in the case of gastro-oesophageal reflux). Treatment of peptic ulcers is slightly different depending whether you are taking non-steroidal anti-inflammatory drugs at the time your ulcer is diagnosed.

69

H. *PYLORI* INFECTION ALONE

Before the discovery of *H. pylori*, patients with peptic ulcers were treated with acid-suppressing drugs such as H_2-receptor antagonists or proton pump inhibitors. These drugs are identical to the ones used to treat gastro-oesophageal reflux discussed on p.47. When given for eight weeks these drugs are very effective at healing the ulcer but they have no effect on the underlying cause, that is, *H. pylori* infection. This means that the ulcer may come back in the future, and in years gone by patients required intermittent treatment for peptic ulcer for many years. Now it is known that if you have a peptic ulcer caused by *H. pylori* then eradication of the bacterium is all that is required. This will not only allow the ulcer to heal, but also prevent it coming back. Acid-suppressing drugs are not usually necessary after a course of eradication treatment unless the ulcer caused some internal bleeding, in which case doctors like to give eight weeks of acid-suppressing treatment as a 'belt and braces' approach.

Modern treatments for *H. pylori* infection consist of three drugs taken together for a week. These are two antibiotics taken with a proton pump inhibitor. Treatment of *H. pylori* infection is described in more detail on p.62.

PATIENTS TAKING NSAIDs

As discussed previously (p.63), patients taking a non-steroidal anti-inflammatory drug (NSAID) may get peptic ulcers as a result of the drugs themselves. These patients may also have *H. pylori* infection, but usually the NSAIDs are the most important factor. If possible, the NSAID treatment should be stopped or substituted for a less damaging treatment such as paracetamol or possibly one of the newer potentially safer NSAIDs. The ulcer itself is treated in traditional fashion with an eight-week course of an acid-suppressing drug such as an H_2-receptor antagonist or proton pump inhibitor. If you are able to stop the NSAID then no further treatment may be required. If you cannot stop your anti-inflammatory treatment, however, you may also be prescribed an acid-suppressing treatment to take long term to prevent your ulcer coming back. Misoprostol is a drug that is sometimes used instead of acid suppression to prevent ulcers in patients on NSAIDs. It helps to boost the defences of the stomach and the duodenum against the damaging effects of the drugs. It is chemically similar to the natural prostaglandin chemicals found in the stomach lining that are inhibited by NSAIDs. Although misoprostol is safe, it does cause diarrhoea in some people, which limits its usefulness. Misoprostol is not given to premenopausal women who are capable of conceiving children as it causes miscarriages.

At the moment doctors do not agree on whether *H. pylori* infection should be treated in patients with ulcers caused by NSAIDs. Some feel that the infection should always be eradicated if an ulcer is present, whether or not patients take NSAIDs. Recent evidence, however, shows that eradicating the infection may make no difference or, worse, may make ulcers more difficult to heal. The current advice is that the infection need not be eradicated, although this advice may change in the future.

DUODENAL AND GASTRIC ULCERS

If you have a duodenal ulcer no further treatment is required. If you have a gastric ulcer, however, the doctor will arrange further tests (usually another endoscopy) to make sure that it has healed after treatment. This is because, very occasionally, cancer cells may be present in a gastric ulcer, preventing it healing.

SURGERY

Before newer treatments became available, surgery was commonly recommended for people with peptic ulcers. These days it is only required to treat some complications of ulcers and, very occasionally, when ulcers do not respond to treatment. There are many different operations available, but the general aim of surgical treatment is to reduce the acid secretion of the stomach glands by cutting the nerves that supply the stomach (a procedure known as a vagotomy). Another consequence of a vagotomy is that the stomach cannot empty properly afterwards so, in addition, the surgeon performs an operation on the stomach itself to correct this.

CONCLUSION

Peptic ulcers are reasonably common and, if your doctor suspects an ulcer is the cause of your symptoms, the best way to confirm the diagnosis is for you to have an endoscopy. The most common cause of peptic ulcer is infection with *Helicobacter pylori*, and eradication of this infection with antibiotics is often all that is required to heal the ulcer. The other main cause of peptic ulcers is treatment with non-steroidal anti-inflammatory drugs (called NSAIDs). Newer NSAIDs are now being produced that may not have this side-effect. Peptic ulcers can nearly always be healed with drugs and surgery is only very rarely necessary. One complication of peptic ulcers is bleeding, so you should consult your doctor immediately if you vomit blood or pass black, tarry motions.

KEY POINTS

- Peptic ulcers can be healed by a course of acid-suppressing drug treatment.

- Once a peptic ulcer is diagnosed, it is important to treat the underlying cause.

- Anti-inflammatory drug treatment should be stopped until the ulcer is healed.

- If *Helicobacter* infection is present, it will be eradicated with antibiotics to prevent the ulcer recurring.

- Surgery is reserved for ulcers that do not heal with drug treatment and for complicated ulcers.

Non-ulcer dyspepsia

Your doctor is likely to diagnose this condition if you have indigestion-type symptoms but tests show that your stomach and duodenum are normal, that is, there is no evidence of ulceration or gastro-oesophageal reflux.

ABDOMINAL PAINS
The main symptoms of non-ulcer dyspepsia are a burning sensation and aching in the upper abdomen.

There is no diagnostic test for non-ulcer dyspepsia so, before it is diagnosed, other conditions causing similar symptoms usually need to be ruled out, either by a physical examination or by other tests. Conditions that may masquerade as non-ulcer dyspepsia are shown in the box opposite.

The main symptoms of non-ulcer dyspepsia are burning and aching in the upper abdomen, which are usually related in some way to eating (food makes it either better or worse), and occasionally nausea. In addition many people suffer from what is often called a 'nervous stomach': their symptoms are often worse at times of stress. It is not known what causes non-ulcer dyspepsia, but there are likely to be many causes. One theory is that, for some reason, the stomachs of people with this condition are much

Conditions to be Ruled Out

There is no specific test for non-ulcer dyspepsia, so before making a firm diagnosis your doctor needs to rule out some other conditions that have similar symptoms.

GALLSTONES: stones that may vary in size from that of small pieces of gravel to 2–3 centimetres in diameter and consist of cholesterol and the breakdown products of red blood cells. They form in the gallbladder and irritate its lining, especially after you have eaten a fatty meal, when the gallbladder contracts and causes pain. Sometimes they may get stuck in the bile duct and cause jaundice.

IRRITABLE BOWEL SYNDROME: this is a very common condition that is associated with muscle spasm within the walls of the intestines. The cause is unknown but the symptoms often seem to be related to stress in many people.

Pain may also come from the muscles of the abdominal wall or from the lower ribs.

more sensitive to stimuli such as normal stomach acid and certain food-stuffs. Another theory suggests that, particularly in people with a 'nervous stomach', the muscles of the stomach wall become especially tense at times of stress, so making the symptoms worse.

From a strictly medical point of view, non-ulcer dyspepsia is never a serious condition, but it can be a severe nuisance. It is important to be sure that it really is the true cause of a person's symptoms. In particular, it very rarely causes weight loss so, if you have indigestion and are losing weight at the same time, your doctor needs to look for other, possibly more serious, causes for your symptoms. If you are taking non-steroidal anti-inflammatory drugs (NSAIDs), your doctor also needs to rule out peptic ulceration before diagnosing non-ulcer dyspepsia.

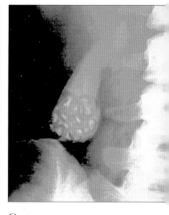

GALLSTONES
This X-ray image shows gallstones. Stones form in the gallbladder and irritate its lining, especially after a fatty meal.

SELF TREATMENT

The most important step is to understand the condition and realise that your symptoms are not the result of something more serious. The next step is to try to alter any aspects of your lifestyle that are likely to be making your symptoms worse. Generally speaking, the most important changes that you can make towards achieving a healthier way of living are to stop smoking, lose weight if necessary and make sure that you are eating the right kind of diet (see p.17). The most common culprits when it comes to making this kind of indigestion worse are fatty or fried foods, hot and spicy foods, certain vegetables such as onions and tomatoes and occasionally caffeine in the form of tea, coffee and cola-type drinks. If you find that any of these things upset you, cut them out and also make a point of increasing your daily intake of high-fibre foods. This not only often helps to relieve symptoms of non-ulcer dyspepsia but also helps to protect you against many other conditions such as heart disease, high blood pressure and bowel cancer. Suitable fibre is found in fruit and vegetables, high-fibre breakfast cereals and whole-grain bread.

MEDICAL TREATMENT

There is no true drug 'panacea' for non-ulcer dyspepsia. Certain drugs are effective, but they are usually prescribed only for people whose symptoms are still intolerable even though they have followed all the lifestyle advice given above.

Unlike the acid-related disorders of peptic ulcer and gastro-oesophageal reflux, non-ulcer dyspepsia does not usually respond to treatment with antacid medication.

The drugs that are most effective are usually those that alter the way the stomach empties itself. Examples of these 'prokinetic' drugs, which are only available on prescription, are domperidone, metoclopramide and cisapride (see p.49). Tablets are taken half an hour before meals to help the stomach muscles coordinate correctly, thus reducing symptoms of tension in the stomach wall and nausea. Treatment with these drugs often has to be continued for several months, so knowing about possible side-effects is important. As these drugs have an effect on the movement not only of the stomach but also of the intestine, they sometimes cause crampy lower abdominal pain and diarrhoea. Generally they are safe, but more severe side-effects can occur – in particular metoclopramide is not usually given to young women and children because it can cause neck and face muscle spasms known as a dystonic reaction (this side-effect is much less common in men and older women).

CONCLUSION

Non-ulcer dyspepsia is very common and, although often uncomfortable, is not serious. Symptoms of upper abdominal discomfort and nausea can often be easily controlled by lifestyle changes such as stress reduction, stopping smoking, weight loss and healthier eating. A minority of people who still have severe symptoms despite lifestyle changes may need treatment with prokinetic drugs. Non-ulcer dyspepsia should not be confused with more serious conditions requiring different treatment. If you are losing weight (and have done so without trying) or if you are taking NSAIDs and develop new indigestion symptoms, you should see your doctor.

KEY POINTS

- Non-ulcer dyspepsia is one of the most common causes of indigestion and is never serious.

- Treatment is based on understanding the condition and making lifestyle changes, such as avoiding certain foods that make it worse.

Stomach cancer

Stomach cancer, although much less common than the other causes of indigestion, is an extremely serious condition that must be diagnosed early on if treatment is to be effective.

The cancer actually develops in cells lining the stomach, called glandular cells. If untreated, the cancer can then spread to involve the whole thickness of the stomach and, via the bloodstream, the liver. This process can occur relatively quickly, which is why the condition is so difficult to treat unless picked up early on.

Although the person concerned may consult their doctor because of a burning upper abdominal pain (similar to that caused by a peptic ulcer), cancer usually causes more of an ache and the person may often be off food and feel very full after even quite small meals. As a result of the loss of appetite, weight loss is common. The combination of these symptoms should always be taken seriously and should always be assessed by a doctor.

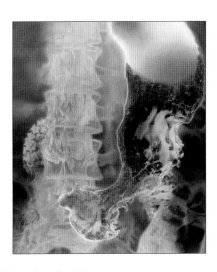

CANCER OF THE STOMACH
In this X-ray, barium has been used to outline the stomach (seen as pink). The right-hand edge of the stomach is uneven where a tumour is growing in the stomach wall.

CAUSES OF STOMACH CANCER

The actual cause of stomach cancer is not known and it may be the result of a variety of factors. There are no proven genetic links and it is more likely that stomach cancer is caused by environmental factors. Certainly, stomach cancer is more common in some countries than others – it is much more common in the Far East than in Europe and this may be caused by, among other things, a difference in diet between the two populations. It is known that the descendants of Japanese emigrants to the West have the same incidence of stomach cancer as Westerners, supporting the influence of environment over genetics. Some scientists believe that long-standing *H. pylori* infection may be an important environmental factor causing stomach cancer, although this is controversial. Even if *H. pylori* infection were important, it is not known whether eradication of the infection would actually lead to a decreased risk of stomach cancer; currently, the medical authorities in the UK and the USA do not recommend treatment for this purpose, although the position may change in the future. Fortunately, the incidence of stomach cancer in Europe and the West is decreasing, although again this is unexplained. Stomach cancer is usually a disease of late middle-aged and elderly people, although it may rarely occur in people under 40.

How Is It Diagnosed?

Diagnosis normally happens when an endoscopy test is done, although cancer may be diagnosed with a barium X-ray. As effective treatment is available only if the disease is caught early, anyone with indigestion who also has the 'sinister' symptoms of lack of appetite and weight loss will need to be thoroughly investigated. As stomach cancer is more common in those aged over 40, full investigation is usually a good idea in anyone over this age who has indigestion for the first time, with or without sinister symptoms.

IS THERE A CURE?

The only curative treatment is an operation to remove the stomach and all the cancer. This is most effective when the disease is in its early stages, hence the need for an early diagnosis and the importance of taking seriously such symptoms as weight loss and feeling full after eating a small amount. Sometimes, the surgeon may be able to leave part of the stomach in place; otherwise, food will have to go directly from the oesophagus to the small intestine after the operation. This means that the person will then have to eat little and often and may well need to take food supplements because digestion is impaired.

If the cancer is small and the surgeon can remove it all then the chance of a long-term cure is very good, but the disease is often advanced at the time of diagnosis and surgery is not possible. Currently, if surgery is not possible or is unsuccessful, then other forms of treatment are very unlikely to result in a cure. The other forms of treatment, such as chemotherapy and laser therapy, do, however, have a very valuable role in controlling uncomfortable symptoms and may prolong life considerably.

CONCLUSION

As treatment for advanced stomach cancer is often unsatisfactory, it is very important to make the diagnosis early on in the course of the disease. Weight loss, loss of appetite and new symptoms in someone aged over 40 may be signs of early stomach cancer and should always be assessed by a doctor. In the future, when the cause of the disease is better understood, the emphasis will be placed more on prevention of stomach cancer, but currently efforts are continually being made to improve non-surgical treatments such as chemotherapy.

POINTS TO REMEMBER

The aim of this book is to help you to understand the causes of indigestion so that you have confidence to be able to decide on the most appropriate course of action.

The most important question when treating your own symptoms is whether an expert opinion is required to rule out a serious condition that requires further investigation. Throughout the book we have tried to highlight those symptoms that are 'sinister' and always require medical advice from the outset:

- Unexplained weight loss.
- Loss of appetite.
- Difficulty swallowing.
- Vomiting blood or material that looks like coffee grounds.
- Passing altered blood in the motions – this makes your stools look 'tarry'.
- Indigestion when you are taking non-steroidal anti-inflammatory drugs.

Indigestion without these sinister symptoms can sensibly be treated at home in the first instance by taking appropriate lifestyle measures – lose some weight, stop smoking and change your diet.

If these measures are not effective, the next step is to try antacids. The easiest and best source of initial advice about antacids is your local pharmacist, who will have a full knowledge about the causes, and treatment, of indigestion. If these simple measures provide symptomatic relief then it may not be necessary to see your doctor but, if symptoms remain after treating yourself for two weeks, or if you are over 40 and develop symptoms for the first time, then it is always wise to seek medical advice.

KEY POINTS

- Stomach cancer is very rare under the age of 40.

- New symptoms after the age of 40, or sinister symptoms such as unexplained weight loss and loss of appetite, should always be discussed with a doctor.

- Stomach cancer can only be diagnosed using hospital-based tests.

Useful addresses

British Society of Gastroenterology
3 St Andrews Place
Regents Park
London NW1 4LB
Tel: (020) 7387 3534
Most British gastroenterologists
(specialists in digestive diseases)
belong to this Society.

Digestive Disorders Foundation
3 St Andrews Place
Regents Park
London NW1 4LB
Tel: (020) 7486 0341
This charitable organisation was founded
to support research into diseases of the
gut. The foundation has leaflets and
booklets about many disorders of the
digestive system which are available
to patients.

**IBS Network – The Irritable Bowel
Syndrome Network**
Members receive a quarterly newsletter –
Gut Reaction –which is written and read
by sufferers of IBS. Members also receive
a 'Can't Wait Card'.
Tel: (0114) 261 1531 (answerphone).

Index

A

abdominal pains 8
  non-ulcer dyspepsia 74
  peptic ulcers 55–6
  stomach cancer 79
acid-suppressing drugs 22–3
  Helicobacter pylori infection
  57, 62, 70
acid/pepsin mixtures 42
addresses 84
age
  angina 41
  Barrett's oesophagus 45
  indigestion 27, 28
  stomach cancer 80
alcohol 17, 18, 43
Algicon 21
alginates 21
alverine citrate 21
anaesthesia 32–3
  intravenous sedation 33, 35
  throat spray 32
angina pain 41
antacids 19–20, 23, 47
anti-arthritic drugs 63–4
anti-inflammatory treatment 71
anti-reflux surgery 51
antibiotics 57, 62
antibody blood test 38
antispasmodics 21–2
appetite loss 26, 79, 80
arthritis 63–4
aspirin 16

B

barium X-rays 29, 35–6, 46
  peptic ulcers 69
  stomach cancer 80
Barrett's oesophagus 45–6, 53
belching 8

biopsies 30
biopsy urease tests 36–7
bleeding 65–6
blood
  loss 26
  tests 29
  vomiting 26
British Society of
  Gastroenterology 61, 84
burping 8

C

caffeine 17, 76
Campylobacter pylori 57
  see also Helicobacter pylori
cancer 41
  see also stomach cancer
catheters, oesophageal
  strictures 52
chemotherapy 81
chest pains 8, 40–1
cimetidine 23
constipation 36
Crohn's disease 65
cyclo-oxygenase 2 inhibitors 64

D

diagnosis, early 28
diaphragm hiatus 43
diarrhoea, traveller's 48
diet 17, 76
  food supplements 81
  modifications of 43, 52, 77
digestive system 10–15
  problems with 13–14
dilators, oesophageal strictures
  52
dimethicone 20
doctors, advice 25–39
drug regimens 62

duodenal ulcers 55, 71–2
duodenum 42
  peptic ulcers 55
dystonic reactions 50, 77

E

emergency surgery 66
emotional stress 14, 74, 75
endoscopy 28, 29–35, 37
  anaesthesia 32–3
  gastro-oesophageal reflux 51
  oesophageal strictures 52
  peptic ulcers 72
  safety of 34–5
environmental factors 80
exercise 17

F

famotidine 23
'fast track' endoscopy 31
fibreoptic instruments 29
food 7
  digestion 10–15
  supplements 81

G

gallstones 14
gas 8
gastric
  atrophy 49
  ulcers 55, 71–2
gastritis 37, 57
gastro-intestinal reflux 69
gastro-oesophageal reflux 8, 14
  causes 41–3
  complications 51–3
  hiatus hernia 43, 44
  sphincter muscle problems
  43–4
  surgery 50–1

symptoms 40–1
treatment of 46–7
gastro-oesophageal valve 42
Gastrocote 21
gastroenteritis 48
gastrointestinal endoscopy 69
gastroscopy *see* endoscopy
Gaviscon 21
glandular cells 79
gullet *see* oesophagus

H

heart disease 20
heartburn 8, 14, 40–54
see also gastro-oesophageal
reflux
Helicobacter pylori 14, 28, 29
antibody blood test 38
biopsy urease test 36–7
consequences of infection
58–61
eradication of 62–3
infection 58, 69, 70
peptic ulcers 56–68
treatment recommendations
61
treatment side-effects 62–3
urea breath test 37–8
vaccination 63
hiatus hernia 43, 44
see also gastro-oesophageal
reflux
high blood pressure 20
hospital referral 27
hydrochloric acid 41
hydrogen-receptor antagonists
see acid-suppressing drugs

I

indigestion
remedies 19–24
self-help measures 16–24
symptoms 7–9
intestines 13
intravenous sedation 33, 35
irritable bowel syndrome 14

K

'keyhole' surgery 50
kidney disease 20

L

lansoprazole 47, 62
large intestines 13
laser treatment 53, 81
lifestyle factors 17, 43
non-ulcer dyspepsia 76
peptic ulcers 69
liver 79
lower oesophageal sphincter
muscle, problems with 43–4
lymphoma 61, 65

M

medical advice 25–39
minor symptoms 7
Misoprostol 71
monitoring clip 33
mucus layer defence system 64
muscular pains 63

N

National Institutes of Health in
the USA 61
nausea 39, 56, 74
'nervous stomach' 50, 74, 75
non-steroidal anti-
inflammatory drugs
(NSAIDs) 16–18, 75
peptic ulcers 63–4, 69, 70–1
non-ulcer dyspepsia 14
Helicobacter pylori infection 60
medical treatment 76–7
self treatment 76
symptoms 28, 74–5
NSAIDs *see* non-steroidal anti-
inflammatory drugs

O

oesophagitis 44, 51, 52
oesophagus 12, 42
abnormalities of 35

cancer of 45, 53
narrowing and scarring of
52–3
strictures 44–5, 52–3
omeprazole 47, 62
'open access' endoscopy 31
outpatients, barium X-rays
35–6
over-indulgence 7
over-the-counter remedies
19–24
oxygen levels 31

P

pain
abdominal 55–6, 74, 79
angina 41
indigestion 8
pantoprazole 47
paracetamol 18
peppermint oil 21
pepsin 41
peptic ulcers
alternative causes 63–5
causes 56–65
complications 65–7
diagnosis 27–8
disease tests 36
Helicobacter pylori 57–63
surgery 72
symptoms 55–6
treatment 69–73
perforation 66
peritonitis 66
personal hygiene 58
pharmacist 7
advice 18–19
physical examinations 27
premenopausal women 71
prokinetic drugs 47, 49–50
side-effects 77
prostaglandins 64
proton pump inhibitors 47–8,
57, 70
side-effects 48, 52
therapy 37, 38

pulse 31
pyloric stenosis 66–7

R

radiation 37–8
radiologists 36
ranitidine 23
referral to hospital 27
regurgitation 40
remedies 16–24

S

saliva production 10–11
screening programmes 53
seaweed *see* alginates
Second World War 58
sedation, intravenous 33, 35
sinister symptoms 25–6, 28, 80
small intestines 13
smoking 24, 43, 44, 56, 65, 69,
    76, 77
socially disadvantaged people
    56
sphincter muscle problems
    43–4
stomach
    acid 14, 48
    acid neutralising effect 60
    cancer 14
    functions 12–13
    nervous 50, 74, 75
    peptic ulcers 55–68
    thinning of lining 49, 60

tumours 61
ulcers 14
stomach cancer
    causes 79–80
    curative treatment 81
    diagnosis 80, 81
    Helicobacter pylori infection
        60–1, 67
    symptoms 79
stomach lining specimens 36
stomach lymphoma 61
stools, blood in 26
stress 56, 74, 75
    reduction 77
surgery
    gastro-oesophageal reflux
        50–1
    stomach cancer 81
swallowing, difficulties 26, 40,
    45
symptom changes 45

T

telescope test *see* endoscopy
tests 28–39
    barium X-rays 29
    blood 29
    endoscopy 29–35
    Helicobacter pylori 29, 36–40
throat spray 32
tissue samples *see* biopsies
traveller's diarrhoea 48
treatment, failure to respond 28

U

ulcers
    duodenal 55, 71–2
    gastric 55, 71–2
    healing drugs 69
    peptic 55–73
    stomach 14
unusual symptoms 27
upper gastrointestinal
    endoscopy 46
upper intestinal tract 55
upper intestine, *see also*
    duodenum
urea breath test 37–8, 62
useful addresses 84

V

vagotomy 72
video cameras 30, 51
vomiting blood 26, 66

W

weight 17, 43, 51
weight loss
    gastro-oesophageal reflux 52
    non-ulcer dyspepsia 75, 77
    sinister symptoms 26
    stomach cancer 79, 80
wind 8

Z

Zollinger–Ellison syndrome 65

Acknowledgements

PUBLISHER'S ACKNOWLEDGEMENTS
Dorling Kindersley would like to thank the following for their help
and participation in this project:

Design Assistance Chris Walker; **Production** Michelle Thomas;
DTP Jason Little; **Consultancy** Dr. Sue Davidson;
Indexing Indexing Specialists, Hove; **Administration** Christopher Gordon

Illustrations (p.20, p.21, p.42, p.48, p.49) © Dave Eastbury; (p.30) Richard Tibbetts;
(p.59) Debbie Maizels

Picture Research Andy Sansom; **Picture Librarian** Charlotte Oster.

PICTURE CREDITS
The publisher would like to thank the following for their kind
permission to reproduce their photographs. Every effort has been made
to trace the copyright holders. Dorling Kindersley apologises for any
unintentional omissions and would be pleased, in any such cases,
to add an acknowledgement in future editions.

Sally and Richard Greenhill p.64; **Image Bank** p.25 (Romilly Lockyer), p.2;
Science Photo Library p.8 (Will and Deni McIntyree),
p.10, p.35, p.29 (Dr. Klaus Shiller), p.40 (P. Hawtin), pp.3 & 55 (Dr. B. Gabel CNRI),
p.69 (Simon Fraser), p.75 (Gca-CNRI), p.79 (Salisbury District Hospital).